YOU'RE THE CHEF

PERFECT PIZZA RECIPES

Jennifer S. Larson Photographs by B

MILLBROOK PRESS • MINNEAPOLIS

For my pizza-loving kids, Isaiah and Grace —J.S.L.

For Dr. Devine and Dr. Schroeder —B.C.

Photography by Brie Cohen
Food in photographs prepared by chef David Vlach
Illustrations by Laura Westlund/Independent Picture Service
The image on page 5 is used with the permission of © iStockphoto.com/stuartbur.

Allergy alert: The recipes in this book contain ingredients to which some people can be allergic. Anyone with food allergies or sensitivities should follow the advice of a physician or other medical professional.

Millbrook Press
A division of Lerner Publishing Group, Inc.
241 First Avenue North
Minneapolis, MN 55401 U.S.A.

Website address: www.lernerbooks.com

Main body text set in Fellbridge Standard.
Typeface provided by Monotype Typography.

Library of Congress Cataloging-in-Publication Data

Larson, Jennifer S., 1967– author.
Perfect pizza recipes / by Jennifer Larson ; photographs by Brie Cohen.
pages cm — (You're the chef) Includes index.
ISBN 978–0–7613–6637–9 (lib. bdg. : alk. paper)
1. Pizza—Juvenile literature. I. Cohen, Brie, illustrator. II. Title.
TX770.P58L37 2013
641.82'48—dc23 2012020924

Manufactured in the United States of America
1 – BP – 12/31/12

TABLE OF CONTENTS

It's pizza time! Get ready for some delicious favorites like cheese and pepperoni, plus some surprises like breakfast pizza. YOU can be the chef and make food for yourself and your family. Follow these recipes for some delicious meals. And maybe you'll even add some favorite toppings of your own!

I developed these recipes with the help of my kids, who are seven and ten years old. They can't do all the cooking on their own yet, but they can do a lot.

Can't get enough of cooking? Check out www.lerneresource.com for bonus recipes, healthful eating tips, links to cooking technique videos, metric conversions, and more!

BEFORE YOU START

Reserve your space! Always ask for permission to work in the kitchen.

Find a helper! You will need an adult helper for some tasks. Talk with this person to decide what steps you can do on your own and what steps the adult will help with.

Make a plan! Read through the whole recipe before you start cooking. Do you have the ingredients you'll need? If you don't know what a certain ingredient is, see page 31 to find out more. Do you understand each step? If you don't understand a technique, such as *preheat* or *slice*, turn to page 7. At the beginning of each recipe, you'll see how much time you'll need to prepare the recipe and to cook it. The recipe will also tell you how many servings it makes. Small drawings at the top of each recipe let you know what major kitchen equipment you'll need—such as a stovetop, a toaster, or a microwave.

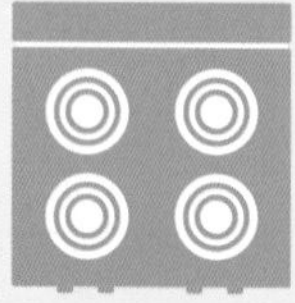
stovetop

toaster

knives

microwave

oven

Wash up! Always wash your hands with soap and water before you start cooking. And wash them again after you touch raw eggs, meat, or fish.

Get it together! Find the tools you'll use, such as measuring cups or a mixing bowl. Gather all the ingredients you'll need. That way you won't have to stop to look for things once you start cooking.

SAFETY TIPS

That's sharp! Your adult helper needs to be in the kitchen when you are using a knife, a grater, or a peeler. If you are doing the cutting, use a cutting board. Cut away from your body, and keep your fingers away from the blade.

That's hot! Be sure an adult is in the kitchen if you use the stove or the oven. Your adult helper can help you cook on the stove and take hot things out of the oven.

Tie it back! If you have long hair, tie it back or wear a hat. If you have long sleeves, roll them up. You want to keep your hair and clothing out of the food and away from flames or other heat sources.

Turn that handle! When cooking on the stove, turn the pot handle toward the back. That way, no one will accidentally bump the pot and knock it off the stove.

Wash it! If you are working with raw eggs or meat, you need to keep things extra clean. After cutting raw meat or fish, wash the knife and the cutting board right away. They must be clean before you use them to cut anything else.

Go slowly! Take your time when you're working. When you are doing something for the first time, such as peeling or grating, be sure not to rush.

Above all, have fun!

Finish the job right!

One of your most important jobs as a chef is to clean up when you're done. Wash the dishes with soap and warm water. Wipe off the countertop or the table. Put away any unused ingredients. The adults in your house will be more excited for you to cook next time if you take charge of cleaning up.

COOKING TOOLS

TECHNIQUES

bake: to cook in the oven

chop: to cut food into small pieces using a knife

discard: to throw away or put in a compost bin. Discarded parts of fruits and vegetables and eggshells can be put in a compost bin, if you have one.

drain: to pour the liquid off of a food. You can drain food by pouring it into a colander or strainer. If you are draining water or juice from canned food, you can also use the lid to hold the food back while the liquid pours out.

grate: to use a food grater to shred food into small pieces

grease: to coat a pan in oil or butter so baked food won't stick to the bottom

knead: to mix dough by hand until it is smooth and stretchy

mix: to stir food using a spoon or fork

preheat: to turn the oven to the temperature you will need for baking. An oven takes about 15 minutes to heat up.

serrated: a tool, such as a knife, that has a bumpy edge

set aside: to put nearby in a bowl or plate or on a clean work space

slice: to cut food into thin pieces

sprinkle: to scatter on top

thaw: to warm frozen food until it is soft

whisk: to stir quickly with a fork or whisk

MEASURING

To measure **dry ingredients**, such as sugar or flour, spoon the ingredient into a measuring cup until it is full. Then use the back of a table knife to level it off. Do not pack it down unless the recipe tells you to. Do not use measuring cups made for liquids.

When you're measuring a **liquid**, such as milk or water, use a clear glass or plastic measuring cup. Set the cup on the table or a counter and pour the liquid into the cup. Pour slowly and stop when the liquid has reached the correct line.

Don't measure your ingredients over the bowl they will go into. If you accidentally spill, you might have way too much!

makes one 12-inch pizza crust

preparation time: 20 minutes
baking time: 15 to 20 minutes

ingredients:

1 cup warm water
1 tablespoon active dry yeast
1 teaspoon sugar
2½ cups all-purpose flour, plus 1 to 3 tablespoons for kneading
3 tablespoons olive oil or vegetable oil
1 teaspoon salt

equipment:

food thermometer (optional)
liquid measuring cup
small bowl
2 spoons
measuring cups—1/4 cup, 1/2 cup, 1 cup
table knife
large bowl
measuring spoons
mixing spoon
12-inch pizza pan or baking sheet
plastic wrap (optional)
small rolling pin (optional)

Homemade Pizza Dough

Make your own pizza crust from scratch! This dough is super fun to make—and super tasty. You can use it for many of the pizza recipes in this book. Or bake it with your own favorite toppings.

1. Prepare the yeast mixture. Turn the sink faucet to warm. **Put** the inside of your wrist under the running water. It should feel a little warm on your wrist, but *not* hot. Hot water will kill the yeast. (If you have a food thermometer, you can use it to check the temperature of the water. It should be between 105°F and 115°F.) Measure ¼ cup warm water and **pour** it into a small bowl. **Put** the yeast into the water and **stir**. **Add** the sugar. Let the yeast stand for about 10 minutes. The yeast and water mixture should start to get foamy. If it doesn't get foamy, the water could be too hot or cold. Or the yeast may be too old. Try repeating the steps above with yeast from a new packet or jar.

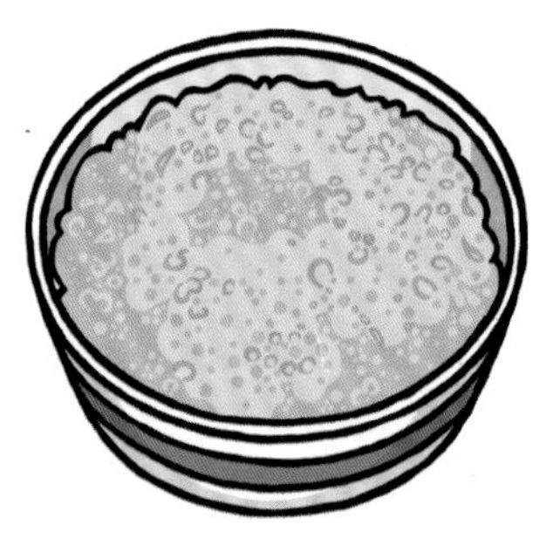

2. Measure 2½ cups flour. Use a spoon to **scoop** flour into the measuring cup. Scrape any extra flour off the top of the measuring cup with a table knife. Do not pack the flour into the cup, or you will have too much. **Pour** flour into a large bowl.

Turn the page for more Homemade Pizza Dough

A note about yeast:

Did you know that yeast is alive? Yeast is a tiny organism, or living creature. Yeast helps dough rise, or expand, by making bubbles in the dough. Yeast grows in warm temperatures but dies if it gets too hot. It also likes to eat sugar. When you add warm water and sugar to the yeast, you will see foamy bubbles form as it grows. (If you don't see foam, the yeast might be too old. Or you might have added water that's too hot or cold.)

3. **Add** 2 tablespoons of oil, ¾ cup warm water, salt, and yeast mixture to the flour. Use a mixing spoon to **stir** the flour mixture until it is doughy and hard to stir. **Spread** 1 tablespoon of flour onto a clean surface, such as a table or counter. This flour will keep the dough from sticking to the table. Then, with clean, dry hands, take the dough out of the bowl. **Place** the dough on the floured surface so you can knead it. If the dough sticks to your hands, put some flour on your hands.

4. Next, knead the dough. Gather it into a ball and **push** it down with your hands. **Fold** the dough in half. With the heel of your hand, **press** down and forward so that you are flattening and stretching the dough at the same time. **Turn** the dough a quarter turn and repeat the folding, flattening, and stretching steps. Keep turning and kneading the dough for about 5 minutes. You can **add** more flour to the surface or your hands if the dough gets sticky. **Add** as little additional flour to the dough as possible to avoid making it too tough. The dough should be smooth and stretchy when you're done. Let the dough rest for another 5 minutes.

5. While the dough is resting, **grease** a baking sheet or pizza pan with 1 tablespoon oil. Use a piece of plastic wrap or your hands to **spread** it around.

6. **Spread** the dough onto the pan, stretching and pushing it with your hands until it covers the pan. You can also use a small rolling pin.

7. Your pizza dough is now ready for toppings. You can use it for many of the recipes that follow in this book. Or make up your own recipe. Either way, it should be baked at 450°F for 15 to 20 minutes.

TRY THIS!

For a **healthier** pizza, try making a crust with **whole-wheat** flour. Replace the 2½ cups of white flour in this recipe with 1½ cups white flour and 1 cup **whole wheat flour**.

makes one 12-inch pizza crust

preparation time: 15 minutes
baking time: 15 to 20 minutes

ingredients:

2 cups biscuit mix
½ cup water

equipment:

spoon
measuring cup—1 cup
table knife
large bowl
liquid measuring cup
large spoon
12-inch pizza pan or
baking sheet
small rolling pin (optional)

Quick Biscuit Pizza Crust

Keep a box of biscuit mix in the cupboard, and you can make this quick pizza dough anytime.

1. **Measure** biscuit mix. Use a spoon to **scoop** biscuit mix into the measuring cup. **Scrape** any extra mix off the top of the measuring cup with a table knife. Do not pack the mix into the cup, or you will have too much. **Put** the mix in a large bowl. Measure the water and **pour** it in the bowl.

2. **Stir** the water and biscuit mix with a large spoon until a dough forms. If the dough becomes too hard to stir, you can use your (clean) hands to mix it. Let the dough rest for about 5 minutes.

TRY THIS!

You can make a **mini pizza** for an after-school snack. To make a pizza for **one** person, use ½ cup of **biscuit mix** and 2 tablespoons **water**.

3. **Spread** the dough onto the pan, stretching and pushing it with your hands until it covers the pan. You can also use a small rolling pin.

4. Your pizza dough is now ready for toppings. You can use it for many of the recipes that follow in this book. Or make up your own recipe. Either way, it should be baked at 450°F for 15 to 20 minutes.

A note about pizza crust:

You can make pizza with all kinds of crusts. Yeast and biscuit doughs take a bit of time to make, but they are super tasty. Most grocery stores also sell frozen or refrigerated pizza dough. Store-bought baked crusts are another quick option. For easy mini pizzas, try English muffins, tortillas, sliced bread, pita bread, or bagels.

In the recipes that follow, you can use any of these crust ideas instead of homemade dough. Just remember, if the crust is already baked, your pizza won't need to stay in the oven as long. Check it often to make sure it doesn't burn. Experiment with different crusts—or dream up your own. Discover what kind you like best!

makes one 12-inch pizza

preparation time: 20 minutes
baking time: 15 to 20 minutes

ingredients:

1 batch pizza dough (see pages 8 to 11 or 12 to 13)
6 ounces (1½ cups) mozzarella cheese
1¼ cups pasta sauce
20 pepperoni slices
grated Parmesan cheese

equipment:

12-inch pizza pan or baking sheet
grater
bowl or plate
spoon or table knife
oven mitts

Classic Pepperoni Pizza

Make your own version of this delicious, classic pizza. Serve it with some carrot sticks and apple slices to make it a well-balanced meal.

1. **Preheat** the oven to 450°F.

2. Prepare pizza dough and **put** it on the pan, as directed in the dough recipe.

3. Use a grater to **grate** mozzarella cheese into a bowl or onto a plate.

4. Use a spoon or table knife to **spread** the sauce on the pizza crust. Be sure to spread it all over, but leave the edges of the crust uncovered. (You might want to put more or less sauce on top. It depends on how thick you like it.)

5. **Sprinkle** cheese on top.

6. **Place** pepperoni slices evenly on the pizza.

7. Use oven mitts to **place** the pizza into the oven. Bake for 15 to 20 minutes, or until the edges of the crust and the cheese begin to turn a golden brown.

8. **Sprinkle** your pizza with a small amount of grated Parmesan cheese, if you like.

serves 4

preparation time: 20 to 25 minutes
cooking time: 15 to 20 minutes

ingredients:

4 sausage links
4 eggs
2 tablespoons milk
1 tablespoon vegetable oil
salt and pepper to taste
2 ounces (½ cup) mozzarella cheese
2 to 4 English muffins
2 tablespoons ketchup (optional)

equipment:

frying pan
spatula
knife
cutting board
medium bowl
fork or whisk
grater
bowl or plate
table knife
measuring spoons
toaster
4 dinner plates
microwave-safe plate

Breakfast Pizza

Start your day with this yummy morning pizza!

1. **Place** sausages in a frying pan. Turn the burner under the pan on medium heat. Cook sausages for about 10 minutes, or follow directions on the package. **Turn** sausages with a spatula until they are brown on all sides. **Remove** from heat. When sausages are cool, use the knife and cutting board to **cut** each one into thin, round slices. **Wash** the frying pan and the spatula.

MEDIUM
LOW
HIGH

2. **Crack** eggs into medium bowl. **Add** milk. **Whisk** with a fork or a whisk until foamy.

3. **Measure** 1 tablespoon vegetable oil and **pour** into the clean frying pan. Use a spatula to **spread** the oil around the pan. Turn the burner under the pan on medium-high heat. Wait 2 to 3 minutes until the oil gets hot. **Add** egg mixture to the pan to make scrambled eggs. Let the eggs cook for about 30 seconds until they begin to set. Then use the spatula to **stir** the eggs and **flip** them over. Keep stirring and flipping the eggs until they are cooked on all sides. They are done when they are no longer wet or gooey. **Sprinkle** some salt and pepper on top.

4. Use a grater to **grate** cheese into a bowl or onto a plate.

5. Take an English muffin out of its package. Use your fingers or a table knife to **separate** the English muffin into 2 halves. (It should come already sliced down the middle.) Place the 2 muffin halves into the toaster. **Toast** them for 2 to 3 minutes, or until they are crunchy and lightly browned. Remove the muffins from the toaster. Repeat with the rest of the English muffins.

6. When all the muffins are toasted, you can get the pizzas ready. Place a muffin on a plate. **Spread** a layer of ketchup on the muffin (if you like ketchup). **Add** eggs and some sausage slices. **Top** with grated cheese. Repeat with the other muffin halves. (The cheese should melt on the warm eggs. If not, put the muffin halves on a microwave-safe plate. Heat for 10 seconds in the microwave.)

7. **Eat** your pizza open-faced. Or add another toasted English muffin on top to make a sandwich. Enjoy!

TRY THIS!

You can add your favorite pizza toppings to this recipe. Try **olives**, **pepperoni** slices, fresh **mushrooms**, or fresh **red** or **green peppers**.

makes one 12-inch pizza

preparation time: 20 to 35 minutes
baking time: 20 minutes

ingredients:

1 batch pizza dough (see pages 8 to 11 or 12 to 13)
2 slices bacon (optional)
1 cup instant potatoes
1 cup water
2 tablespoons butter
½ tablespoon salt
½ cup milk
½ teaspoon garlic powder
1 tomato
1 small stalk broccoli
1 green onion
6 ounces (1½ cups) cheddar cheese

equipment:

12-inch pizza pan or baking sheet
3 paper towels
microwave-safe plate
oven mitts
measuring cups—1/2 cup, 1 cup
liquid measuring cup
measuring spoons
medium microwave-safe bowl
2 spoons
cutting board
serrated knife
knife
grater
bowl or plate
oven mitts

Mashed Potato Pizza

This pizza uses mashed potatoes instead of tomato sauce. Try it. It's tasty!

1. **Preheat** the oven to 450°F.

2. Prepare pizza dough and **put it** on the pan, as directed in the dough recipe.

3. Prepare the optional bacon. First, **place** a paper towel on a microwave-safe plate. Take 2 slices of bacon out of the package and **put** them on the towel. **Place** another paper towel on top of the bacon. Cook the bacon in the microwave on high for 2 to 2½ minutes. The bacon should be brown and crispy. Use oven mitts to **remove** the plate. Let cool.

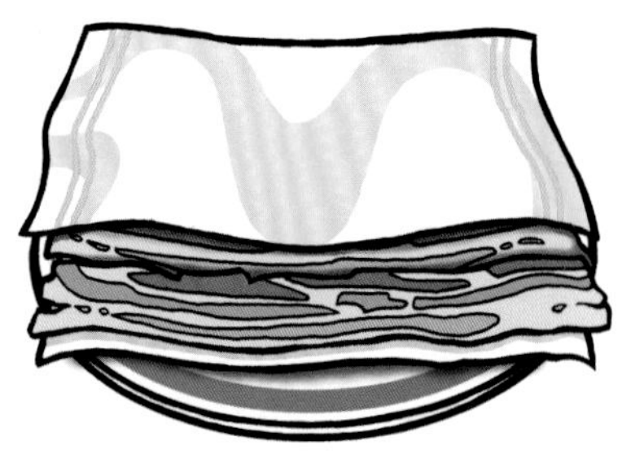

4. Prepare the mashed potatoes. **Add** instant potatoes, water, butter, and salt to a microwave-safe bowl. **Place** in the microwave. Cook on high for 1½ to 2 minutes. Use oven mitts to carefully take the bowl out of the microwave. **Stir** gently.

5. **Wash** the tomato, broccoli, and green onion under cool water. Use the knife and cutting board to cut the vegetables. It works best to cut a tomato with a serrated knife, a knife with bumps along the sharp edge. To cut the tomato, first **cut** out the green or brown circle on the top. Discard it. Then **chop** the rest of the tomato. Cut enough to make about ½ cup.

6. To cut the broccoli, **cut** off the bottom of the stem and discard. Cut the rest of the stem into thin round chunks. If the circles are big, you can cut them into halves or quarters. Then cut the broccoli tops lengthwise into small pieces. Cut enough to make about ½ cup.

Turn the page for more Mashed Potato Pizza

Mashed Potato Pizza continued

7. To cut the green onion, first **cut** off the roots and discard. Remove any dry or wilted green parts. Then **slice** the onions into small pieces about ½ inch long. You can use both the white and green parts of the onion.

8. Use a grater to **grate** the cheese into a bowl or onto a plate.

9. Use a spoon to **scoop** the mashed potatoes onto the pizza crust. **Spread** the potatoes with the back of the spoon. Be sure to spread them all around, but leave the edges of the crust uncovered.

10. **Crumble** the bacon into small pieces. **Sprinkle** it on top of the potatoes.

11. **Sprinkle** the tomato, broccoli, and green onion all over the pizza. **Sprinkle** the top with cheese.

12. Use oven mitts to **place** the pizza into the oven. Bake for 20 minutes, or until the edges of the crust and the cheese on top begins to turn golden brown. Use oven mitts to **remove** the pizza. Serve.

TRY THIS!

This pizza is tasty with **rosemary**, an herb. Try adding ½ teaspoon dried or fresh rosemary in step 11.

Ham and Pineapple Calzone

A calzone is a folded-up pizza. Make some extras and take one to school in your lunch!

serves 4

dough preparation: 30 to 35 minutes
baking time: 15 to 20 minutes

ingredients:

1 batch Homemade Pizza Dough (see pages 8 to 10)
1 8-ounce can pineapple chunks
6 ounces cooked, diced ham
6 ounces (1½ cups) mozzarella cheese
1 to 3 tablespoons flour
1½ cups pasta sauce
1 tablespoon vegetable or olive oil

equipment:

can opener
colander
grater
plate
measuring spoons
rolling pin
ruler
measuring cup—1/4 cup
spoon
baking sheet
plastic wrap (optional)
spatula
oven mitts

1. **Preheat** the oven to 450°F.

2. Prepare Homemade Pizza Dough through step 4. **Divide** dough into 4 equal balls and set aside.

Turn the page for more Ham and Pineapple Calzone

TRY THIS!
You can put any of your favorite pizza toppings inside the calzones. Try preparing small bowls of toppings, and let your friends or family make their own.

3. Use a can opener to **open** the can of pineapple. Put a colander in the sink, and **pour** the pineapple into the colander to drain the liquid.

4. Use a grater to **grate** the cheese onto a plate. Divide the cheese into 4 piles of the same size.

5. **Spread** about 1 tablespoon of flour on a clean surface, such as a table or counter. **Place** a ball of dough on the floured surface. **Flatten** the dough with your hands or a rolling pin. (If the dough is sticky, rub some flour on your hands and the rolling pin.) Form the dough into a 6-inch circle by **rolling** it from the center out to the edges. Or use your fingers to **stretch** the dough into a circle. Repeat with the other 3 balls of dough.

6. Fill the first calzone. Use a spoon to **spread** ¼ cup pasta sauce plus a little more on half of the dough circle. **Put** ¼ cup of ham and ¼ cup pineapple on the sauce. **Sprinkle** cheese from one of your 4 cheese piles on top.

7. **Fold** the empty half of the calzone over the filling. Then **pinch** the edges together to close. Be sure to seal the edges tightly. Otherwise, the sauce will leak out when the calzone bakes.

8. Repeat steps 6 and 7 with the other 3 balls of dough.

9. **Grease** a baking sheet with 1 tablespoon oil. Use a piece of plastic wrap or your hands to **spread** it around. Carefully **place** each calzone on the baking sheet with your hands or a large spatula.

10. Use an oven mitt to **place** the baking sheet into the oven. Bake for 15 to 20 minutes, or until the crust is golden brown.

serves 4 to 6

preparation time: 30 minutes
baking time: 20 to 25 minutes

ingredients:

1 medium tomato
2 green onions
1 cup frozen corn
1 15-ounce can refried beans
4 ounces (1 cup) Monterey Jack cheese
½ pound ground beef
½ package 1.25-ounce taco seasoning mix
1 tablespoon vegetable oil
4 large flour tortillas
salsa (optional)

equipment:

cutting board
serrated knife
knife
measuring cup—1 cup
microwave-safe bowl
oven mitts
can opener
grater
plate or bowl
frying pan
wooden spoon or spatula
baking sheet
measuring spoons
plastic wrap (optional)

Tasty Tortilla Pizza

All of your favorite taco toppings served on a pizza!

1. **Preheat** the oven to 350°F.

2. **Wash** the tomato and green onions under cool water. Use the knife and cutting board to cut the vegetables. It works best to cut a tomato with a serrated knife, a knife with bumps along the sharp edge. To cut the tomato, first **cut** out the green or brown circle on the top. Discard it. Then **chop** the rest of the tomato.

3. To chop the green onions, first **cut** off the roots and discard. Remove any dry or wilted green parts. Then **slice** the onions into thin circles. You can use both the white and green parts of the onion.

4. **Put** the corn in a microwave-safe bowl. Cook for 1 minute, or until thawed. (The corn does not need to be hot, just not frozen.) Use oven mitts to **remove** the bowl from the microwave.

5. Use a can opener to **open** the can of refried beans.

6. Use a grater to **grate** the cheese onto a plate or into a bowl.

Turn the page for more Tasty Tortilla Pizza

TRY THIS!

You can make this recipe without meat, if you like. Or try adding other taco toppings, such as sliced **black olives**, chopped **avocado** pieces, or chopped **green pepper**. You can also use **corn tortillas** instead of flour tortillas.

7. **Open** the package of ground beef. **Put** the beef in a frying pan, and turn the burner under the pan on medium-high heat. Use a wooden spoon or spatula to **stir** the beef. Cook for about 10 minutes. The beef should be brown all over, not pink. **Stir** in half of the taco seasoning packet. Turn the burner to low. Cook for 2 to 3 more minutes. If there is a lot of juice in the meat, ask an adult to help you **drain** it off into the sink or trash can.

8. **Grease** a baking sheet or pizza pan with 1 tablespoon oil. Use a piece of plastic wrap or your hands to **spread** it around. **Place** 2 tortillas on a baking sheet. Use a spoon to **spread** a layer of refried beans on top of each tortilla. **Sprinkle** half of the ground beef on each tortilla. **Place** another tortilla on top of each one.

9. **Sprinkle** the tomatoes, green onions, and corn on top of each tortilla. Then **top** with the cheese.

10. Use oven mitts to **place** the baking pan into the oven. Bake for 20 to 25 minutes, until the cheese on top is golden brown. Use oven mitts to **remove** the pan from the oven.

11. **Cut** each tortilla into triangle slices and top with salsa, if you like. Serve.

Mini Mummy Pizzas

You can make these scary pizzas with a friend for an after-school snack. Or freak out your family and make them for dinner—at Halloween or anytime.

serves 2

preparation time: 15 minutes
cooking time: 1 to 2 minutes

ingredients:

1 bagel or English muffin
2 tablespoons pizza sauce
2 sticks of string cheese
1 whole pitted green or black olive

equipment:

knife
cutting board
table knife
measuring spoons
microwave-safe plate
oven mitts

1. Use your fingers or a knife to **separate** the bagel or English muffin into 2 halves. If the bagel or muffin isn't already cut, ask for an adult's help.

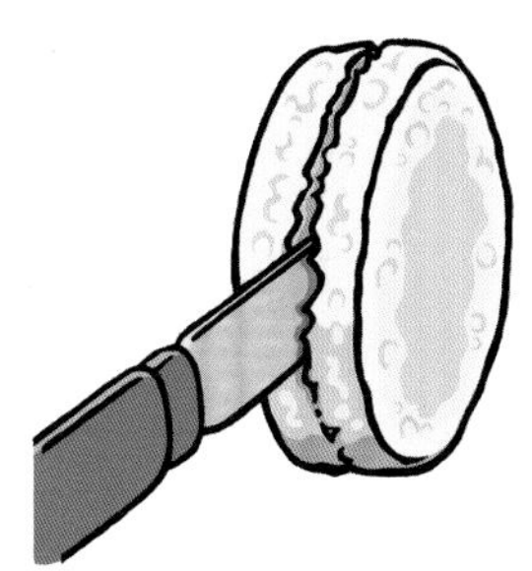

2. Use the table knife to **spread** 1 tablespoon of sauce on half of the bagel or English muffin. Repeat with the other half.

3. **Pull** long strips from a piece of string cheese. **Place** the strips across one of the bagel or muffin halves so it looks like a mummy's face. Leave a little space for the eyes. Repeat with the other half.

4. Use a knife and cutting board to **cut** the olives into 4 circular slices. **Place** 2 olive pieces on each half to make the mummy's eyes.

5. Place the English muffins on a microwave-safe plate. Cook in the microwave for 1 to 2 minutes, or until cheese is melted. Use oven mitts to remove and serve.

serves 6 to 8

preparation time: 25 to 35 minutes
baking time: 10 to 12 minutes

ingredients:

1 frozen or refrigerated piecrust
1 peach
1 kiwi
4 to 5 medium strawberries
1 banana
8 ounces cream cheese
⅓ cup sugar
1 teaspoon vanilla extract

equipment:

knife
cutting board
vegetable peeler (optional)
pie pan
fork
oven mitts
medium microwave-safe bowl
measuring cup—⅓ cup
measuring spoons
mixing spoon
rubber scraper or table knife

Fruit Pizza Delight

Try this delicious fruit pizza for dessert. Have fun decorating it!

1. If the piecrust is frozen, take it out of the freezer and let it **thaw** while you prepare the fruit.

2. **Preheat** the oven to 450°F.

3. **Wash** all fruit except the banana under cool water. Use the knife and cutting board to **cut** the fruit. To cut the peach, lay it on the cutting board. **Cut** down the middle of the fruit from top to bottom. The knife will hit the large pit in the center. Carefully **turn** the peach against the knife to cut a circle all the way around the middle of the fruit. You may need an adult to help you with the cutting. Next, pick up the peach and gently **twist** the two halves in opposite directions until the fruit comes apart. Remove the pit with your fingers or the knife. Lay one half of the peach on its flat side and **cut** into slices. Repeat with the other half. Set aside.

4. To cut the kiwi, first **cut** off the top and bottom of the fruit. You can leave the skin on if you want—it is fine to eat. If you want to **remove** the skin, use a sharp vegetable peeler. Start at the top of the fruit and carefully **peel** down toward the bottom. Repeat this all the way around the fruit. Then use a knife to **slice** the kiwi into round slices.

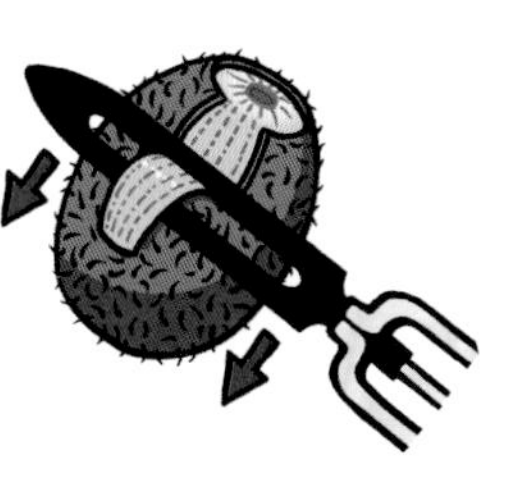

Turn the page for more Fruit Delight Pizza

TRY THIS!

You can add whatever kind of fruit you like to this recipe. Try **blueberries**, sliced **grapes**, **raspberries**, or **pineapple**. Or sprinkle a little **coconut** on top.

5. To cut strawberries, **cut** around the stem of the fruit. Discard the stem. Then cut the strawberry into thin slices. Set aside.

6. **Peel** the banana. **Cut** the banana into round slices.

7. Prepare the piecrust. If the piecrust is rolled up, **unroll** it and place it in the pie pan. Use a fork to **poke** several holes in different places on the bottom of the piecrust.

8. Use oven mitts to **put** the pie pan in the oven. **Bake** for 10 to 12 minutes. The crust should be light brown. Set aside to cool.

9. Place the cream cheese in a microwave-safe bowl. **Heat** in the microwave for about 30 seconds. Use oven mitts to **remove** the bowl from the microwave.

10. **Add** sugar and vanilla to the cream cheese. Use a spoon to **mix** it together well. Put it in the refrigerator to **chill**.

11. When piecrust is completely cool, take the cream cheese mixture out of the refrigerator. Use the rubber scraper or a table knife to **spread** cream cheese mix onto the crust.

12. **Decorate** the pie with your fruit slices. Get creative. Make a colorful pattern—or maybe a face!

13. **Cut** into slices to serve.

SPECIAL INGREDIENTS

basil: fresh or dried leaves from a basil plant. Dried basil is sold at grocery stores in the baking section. Fresh basil is sold at many grocery stores and farmers' markets.

biscuit mix: a mix of dry ingredients used to make biscuits, pancakes, or pizza dough. The mix usually comes in a box and is sold in the baking aisle at most grocery stores.

cooked, diced ham: cooked ham that is already diced. Diced ham is located in the meat or deli section of the grocery store. If you can't find diced ham, look for a package of sliced ham.

instant potatoes: dried, powdered potatoes that usually come in a box. They are usually sold in the pasta and rice aisle at the grocery store.

pasta sauce: a jarred tomato sauce used for spaghetti and other pasta dishes. It can be found in the pasta aisle of the grocery store.

pizza sauce: a canned tomato sauce used for making pizzas. It is usually found in the canned vegetable or pasta aisles in the grocery store.

refried beans: a seasoned, fried, and mashed bean used in many Mexican dishes. Refried beans can be found in the Mexican food section of most grocery stores.

taco seasoning: a packet of spices blended for tacos. Look for taco seasoning in the grocery store—often near the taco shells and salsa.

tortilla: a flat bread that is often served with Mexican foods. Tortillas can be made with white flour, whole wheat flour, ground corn, or other grains. Look for them in the deli or Mexican food section of most grocery stores.

vanilla extract: liquid vanilla flavor. You can find vanilla in the baking section of the grocery store. Most stores sell both pure vanilla extract and artificially flavored extract. Either type will work.

yeast: a tiny organism, or living creature. Yeast gives pizza crust its chewy texture and bready taste. It causes bread loaves to rise by making tiny bubbles as it eats sugar mixed in the flour. You can buy yeast at the grocery store, often in the baking aisle. It comes in packets or a jar. This cookbook uses active dry yeast (not instant yeast, which is also called bread machine yeast).

FURTHER READING AND WEBSITES

ChooseMyPlate.gov
http://www.choosemyplate.gov/children-over-five.html
Download coloring pages, play an interactive computer game, and get lots of nutrition information at this U.S. Department of Agriculture website.

Farmers Markets Search
http://apps.ams.usda.gov/FarmersMarkets/
Visit this site to find a farmers' market near you!

Glaser, Linda. *Garbage Helps Our Garden Grow.* Minneapolis: Millbrook Press, 2010.
This book explains what composting is and how it works.

How Does a Pizza Grow?
http://nationalzoo.si.edu/animals/kidsfarm/PizzaGarden/default.cfm
Learn about where the parts of a pizza come from!

Karmel, Annabel. *Mom and Me Cookbook.* New York: DK Publishing, 2005.
This kid-friendly cookbook includes recipes for pizza and other tasty meals.

Recipes
http://www.sproutonline.com/crafts-and-recipes/recipes
Find more fun and easy recipes for kids at this site.

INDEX